Well Defined
Vocabulary in Rhyme

Michael Salinger

Illustrations by Sam Henderson

ISBN: 978-0-9905435-8-9
Text Copyright © 2009 Michael Salinger
Illustrations Copyright © 2009 Sam Henderson

Red Giant Books
www.redgiantbooks.com

To Stephi, for defining love- M.G.S.

Aggregate believes in group hugs
likes large parties, crowds of all sorts
loves a parade
any great grouping whether matched or mixed
will do the trick
when examined in total
because aggregate is the big picture
the whole ball o' wax
the kit and caboodle
all of Grandma's knick-knacks
a mass
and/or amassed

Aggregate: a collection of objects into a mass

2 **Berate** should hand out earplugs
his lecturing tends to get loud
his criticisms long and severe
he means to demean, that's clear
he tends to go over the top
shouting and scolding with zest
making his victim feel small
is the one thing he does best
needless to say, his friends are far
and few
which just may explain
a thing or two

Berate: to scold for a length of time

Brevity gets right to the point
doesn't dawdle, dicker, or delay
always short and sweet whenever
there is something to say
or do
brevity comes in handy when you
are subject to a chewing out
a bout of the flu
a pain in the neck
or waiting in line for the loo
in fact this poem has gone on so long
that its recital
would no longer qualify
as an example of its title

Brevity: conciseness of expression; short

4   **Capricious** doesn't have a lot to do
with logic so
don't spend too much time trying
to figure him or his next move out
'cause he's more likely to act on a whim
than follow any plausible plan
if you had to guess what he would say
or do next
one answer would be admissible:
capricious is
unpredictable

Capricious: unpredictable; impulsive

Circuitous is one to avoid shortcuts   5
or any sort of straight line
she's not worried about the most direct route
or trying to save any time
rather she'll soak in the scenery
meander, browse, and digress
taking the path less traveled
eventually she'll get where she's going
though she may be the last to arrive
when asked what took her so long
she'll reply
"It was a lovely day for a drive"

Circuitous: having a winding or circular course

6 **Credulity** doesn't check the facts
question authority
or even ask
if what he's being told is true
he'll believe any old story
you care to spin
not the person to rely on
when out and about
mainly because
it doesn't take too much
to take him in

Credulity: willingness to believe on little evidence

Diffident doesn't stick out in a crowd
not very gaudy, not very loud
a mixture of shy sprinkled with unsure
what's lacked in confidence
is made up in demure
won't take a chance
a stab
or a shot
the type of reservation
that would not come in handy
when one's on vacation

Diffident: hesitant or lacking confidence

Dilatory avoids direct confrontation
taking his while to wear someone down
his approach is slow and methodical
rather than through he goes around
he'll come at you from the side
at wasting time he is an expert
he doesn't expect a fight when he arrives
he has a different trick up his sleeve
he hopes his actions cause his opponent
to get really bored and leave

8

Dilatory: causing delay; hesitant

Disingenuous isn't very honest

though she pretends to be utterly sincere
she asks you to judge a book by its cover
while keeping the contents unclear
she'll smile to your face
professing her intention is true
yet all the while aware
that she's full of grade-A baloney
thus, as Holden Caulfield would say,
disingenuous is nothing if not
a phony

Disingenuous: insincere; dishonest

Equivocal won't make a decision
'cause the facts aren't all in place
the data just doesn't stack up
enough to hazard a guess
between this conclusion
or that
in truth the water's quite muddy
when pressed for opinion
equivocal will answer
this situation requires
more study

10

Equivocal: uncertain or confusing

Erratic never follows a pattern

no set route, rhythm, or road
more of a haphazard approach
stuck in random mode
your guess is as good as mine
as to where he'll end up
or even how he'll get there this time
the only thing about erratic
that can be counted on for sure
is that he can't be counted on
now that's a bet that is secure

Erratic: inconsistent; having no set course

Exorbitant is way out of control
knows no reason to act
with moderation, temperance, or restraint
when charging for goods or services
he'll gouge and then declare
that what he asks is fair
even if it's twice
what any bull market
would bear

12

Exorbitant: exceeding appropriate limits

Extenuating brings a note from his mom
keeps an alibi ready just in case
circumstances beyond his control
form the basis of most all his actions
not to be saddled with blame
he can always find a way to explain
how things just aren't his fault
the result
of this over here
or that over there
now it may sound like an excuse
but chances are
he's telling the truth

Extenuating: partially excusing or justifying

14

Fiasco is an utter disaster
if something could go wrong it has
a train off its track
a dam that has burst
a play in which every actor
has forgotten his lines
you would assume that things
couldn't get worse
except the train was carrying poisonous snakes
there was lava behind that dam
and once those actors turn into werewolves
well, you've got a fiasco on your hands

Fiasco: total failure

Florid is most certainly "all that"

and more
never understated, not one to be demure
a flourish, a flurry, drama's her game
whether writing or speaking her methods the same
be big, be flashy, be bold
use curlicues, glitter, and gol d
don't hold back
ornamentation trumps content
it's the packaging that matters
when something needs to be sold

Florid: ornate or flamboyant

16 **Gregarious** knows how to party
he loves hanging out in a crowd
making friends to him—second nature
always in a group when he goes out
he's happy, he's jovial, and he's friendly
a frat boy who has never grown up
your back-slapping buddy
who's a little too loud
but still too much fun
to rebuff

Gregarious: enjoying the company of others

Haphazard needs neither rhyme nor reason
considering order and pattern
a treasonous act
the fact that her socks don't match
her shirt's inside out
both shoes are for left feet
and her hair sprouts from her head
as if randomly seeded
makes no difference to her
'cause if things are asunder
well then
she has succeeded

Haphazard: random; by chance

Hypothetical asks the question "what if"
her comments based on supposition
rather than hard cold facts
not certain to happen thus
anything hypothetical cares to discuss
is more founded in theory
so while her remarks may be possible
and sound logical, even legit
hypothetical has to admit
what she serves for consumption
is totally based on assumption

18

Hypothetical: based on theory or assumption

Incessant just doesn't know when to quit
seemingly having no beginning
or end
that dog barking at all hours of the night
that friend who always borrows money
a toothache, an ulcer, bad dreams
the nagging of a parent or spouse
like water torture
incessant accumulates
overflowing the cup
never giving in
never giving up

Incessant: unending; ceaseless

20 **Inevitable** is impossible to avoid
like some annoying jerk at a party
who has to be dealt with
it's going to happen, you see it coming
no amount of hiding or running
will change this course of destiny
you'll have to accept, one simple fact is
inevitable has a lot in common
with death and taxes

Inevitable: unavoidable; certain

Infiltrate comes uninvited 21
sneaks in through window
or jimmied back door
squeezing through cracks you'd never think
she'd fit
to gather information
or maybe just sit a bit
she's not very flashy
she's not very loud
but she's been known to take notes
while blending in
with the crowd

Infiltrate: to gradually enter

22 **Insidious** sneaks under the door
little by little by little
spreads across the floor like morning fog
he'll stick to your shoes
and follow you like a kid brother
who can't be shook
he's that tickle in the back of your throat
when you absolutely must be quiet
the smell of turpentine
cheesy song you can't get out of your mind
he's nothing but trouble
but he takes
his time

Insidious: sneaky and harmful

Instigate likes to get the ball rolling

she's the very first domino to tip
with a word or a deed
instigate will proceed the commencement
of an action
she'll prod, poke, nudge
she'll throw the switch to get things going
in a boat headed for a waterfall
instigate is the one that's
rowing

Instigate: to influence or encourage

24   **Jubilant** is beyond plain old happy
she's dancing in the street
kissing strangers, hand clapping
on cloud nine
whooping to the sky
winning lottery ticket in hand
out of her mind with delight
if you see jubilant you just might,
without being rude,
describe her as being
in a very, very, very
good mood

Jubilant: extremely happy; celebrating

Kudos loves to give credit

where credit is due
when you've done a good job
he's the one that'll pat on the back
you aced that test, won the game
cut the grass, survived a rabid weasel attack
he is there with a medal, badge
maybe a trophy
to share and point out your glory
kudos gets my endorsement
for being the prince
of positive reinforcement

Kudos: praise; approval; recognition

Lugubrious is, like, really sad
and doesn't care who knows it
wailing, crying, moaning
pulling out his hair
anything to show it
is the end of the world as far as he's concerned
some would say his sorrow
is a bit over the top
but lugubrious believes
tears are best handled
with a mop

Lugubrious: mournful, sad, or gloomy in an
exaggerated way

Magnanimous rises above the fray

never holds a grudge
is generous in every way
courageous, noble, and kind
forgiving for her comes easy
whether to friend or foe
she's the kind of person we'd all like to know
she'll never be petty
on that you can rely
magnanimous is a really swell person
and that ain't no lie

Magnanimous: generous in forgetting insults; forgiving

Martyr goes down with the ship
bleeding out vital fluids for his cause
although while he's being snuffed
he may expect some applause
the absence of gratitude though
allows him to let everyone know
of his sacrifice so unselfish
for there is one thing
that martyr finds dreaded
it's not the suffering he can't take
it's the fact that he's not getting credit

Martyr: hero who suffers or to cause such suffering

Mitigate likes to smooth things over
highlighting reasons for restraint
illuminating circumstances
that may lessen the taint
of an action
so while the ends
may not always justify the means
mitigate asks you consider
a little leniency
in this particular case
'cause the situation
isn't always what it seems

Mitigate: make less severe

30 **Nemesis** lurks round the corner
your name topping her to do list
ready to pounce and oppose anything
that looks as if it just may go
your way
a cut above your basic enemy
Greek goddess namesake
of divine retribution and vengeance
full of incessant cunning
thus
even though
she's out to get you
you may simply have it
coming

Nemesis: opponent or rival who can't be overcome

Novice hasn't quite figured things out yet
you see he's just been sent into the game
doesn't have much experience
but he's more than willing to try just the same
it's not his fault, everyone has to start
somewhere at sometime
and I'm sure he's gonna
get the hang of things
I'm just saying…
I'm glad he's your surgeon
and not mine

Novice: a beginner in any skill

32 **Oblivion** I knew him well
but can't seem to place his face
I thought he lived here
but the house is gone
a smoking hole left in its wake
in fact there isn't any hide or hair
left of old what's-his-name
could someone please give me a hand—
what I was looking for
again?

Oblivion: state of being completely forgotten

Obsolete is absolutely useless
although in the past
he was reasonably handy
time, it kept on ticking and he
just never bothered to adapt
so now he gets passed over
sits in the corner collecting dust
his colors are fading
his chrome has started to rust
but don't feel too bad for obsolete
his future is not completely bleak
as long as he keeps hanging on
eventually he'll become an antique

Obsolete: mno longer useful; outmoded

Pessimism sees the glass half empty
nothing will ever go his way
he won't pet a dog 'cause he's sure it'll bite
won't try skiing, too many broken legs
every cloud is harboring rain
every good deed an ulterior motive
"we're all doomed"
is this guy's rallying cry
no doubt a fairly depressing
way to live one's life
but when one is convinced existence is cursed
it is plainly easier
to always expect the worst

Pessimism: tendency to stress negative views

Petulant is in no mood

unless that mood is BAD
quick to ire, sure to fire
off remarks quite crude
always the first to take offense
petulant's
prime defense:
cop a major attitude
by acting really rude

Petulant: unreasonably irritable; crabby

Pithy gets right to the point
no beating round the bush for her
short and sweet and completely
relevant to the topic at hand
this girl knows what she's talking about
not one to waste words
being concise for her is a snap
this is your go-to gal
when you need a line or a phrase
that cuts through all the crap

Pithy: brief and full of meaning

Quandary can't decide how to act

seems all of the options are bad
this no-win situation can lead to frustration
damned if ya' don't
damned if ya' do
there just ain't no good way to choose
might as well
just flip a coin
when caught
in a Catch-22

Quandary: state of uncertainty; a dilemma

Recalcitrant categorically has little use
for any authority
and makes sure everyone knows it
digging in heels, sneering, or
joining a protest
are just a couple ways she'll show it
her chief means of defense
is to defy
the powers that be
by looking at them straight in the eye
and confidently saying
"You're not the boss of me!"

38

Recalcitrant: resisting authority; hard to control

Recidivism is incapable of staying out
of trouble
committing crimes, for him, is a habit
he promises virtue
but never succeeds, intends to go straight
but his path always leads
to arrest, trial, incarceration
his anarchistic fixations are categorically chronic
in the garden of humanity
this chap is a weed
but what could you expect
from such a bad seed?

Recidivism: repeated or habitual relapse into crime

40   **Redolent** can be an aroma
      exuding an odor of some sort
      a rose by any other name
      smells just as sweet, but just the same
      a skunk could make a similar claim
      though sometimes not a literal scent
      redolent can still give a hint
      toward an object's nature
      whether fragrance or suggestion
      redolent is a description that
      comes in handy
      whenever one smells a rat

Redolent: having or emitting an odor

Refute can stop a speaker dead
in her tracks
like a brick wall popping up
out of nowhere
he will halt an argument before
it even begins
no weapons needed when he attacks
because refute comes armed
simply
with the facts

Refute: to prove false

Reiterate you can say that again!
and she will
sometimes rephrased, sometimes verbatim
but the message remains the same
for you see, reiterate conceives
that once is never enough
to get her message across
it's pretty tough competing
with all the noise of this busy world
so, she believes
a message worth saying
is also worth repeating

42

Reiterate: to say or do again; repeat

Resignation doesn't bother
to put up a fight
speak or stick up for his self
even when he is right
surrender is his usual tactic
resistance is not the game for him
quitting, walking away, throwing hands in the air
are some of his solutions
in fact the only way for him
to make the situation better
is if his quitting
is done via letter

Resignation: the act of giving up or quitting

44   **Skeptical** is not so certain
that what she's being told is the truth
not one to believe the loss of a tooth
will bring in some money
doesn't quite see how her father
walked to school uphill
both ways!
she asks lots of questions
and she's nobody's patsy
pardon me but
is that a toupee?

Skeptical: showing doubt

Squalid might be a slob

if only he cleaned up his act a bit
his hygiene's the worst
his housekeeping sucks
disorder, filth, and disarray is his curse
living in an open sewer
would cause fewer visitors to gag
if cleanliness is next to godliness
as has been said
then squalid
is headed for hell in a handbag

Squalid: filthy

46   **Tacit** may not come right out and say
what's on his mind out loud
but a wink or a nod
maybe an eyebrow raised
will allow one to infer
what's going on inside his head
with a fair amount of precision
it's just his way
without saying a word
of offering an agreement
with surreptitious permission

Tacit: implied or silently understood

Transient just can't stay put

whether the grass is greener

or his feet just itch

he's got to be on the move

he likes to switch his location

the way other folks change socks

one can wonder

why he's so consumed by wanderlust

but it's tough to get an answer

you know

when the person you'd like to question

is always on the go

Transient: staying for a brief time

48   **Transmute** isn't afraid of a little change
        in fact he usually makes things better
        whether form, appearance,
        or nature
        there's always something he can tweak
        for transmute
        a little alteration would never hurt
        whether he is referring to
        his spiritual constitution
        or the even hem of a woman's skirt

Transmute: to change from one form to another

Unctuous is a little bit slimy
kinda smooth, a little greasy
slippery in appearance or texture
and sometimes deed
unctuous would have you deem
that she is made of silk
if she's talking about her dress
well with that I may agree
but if she means the sincerity
of all the things she says
well that I find a little hard to believe

Unctuous: insincere; oily

50 **Verbose** always has something to say
and say, and say, and say
when one word would do
verbose uses two
or three, or four, or five, or six …
one of his favorite tricks
is to just keep prattling on and on
giving his listeners absolutely no choice
because even more than words
verbose is in love with the sound
of his own voice

Verbose: using or containing too many words

Wistful likes to dwell on thoughts 51
especially if the notion is a little bit
sad
he has a permanent boo-boo lip
but on him it doesn't look bad
you will find him musing
if not amusing
but don't you fret
during his times of distress
or when he has a tear in his eye
for wistful is only really happy
when he feels like
he's going to cry

Wistful: sad longing

CPSIA information can be obtained
at www.ICGtesting.com
Printed in the USA
FFOW02n1813280916
28055FF